# Clumsy Eagle

Level 6F

Written by Melanie Hamm
Illustrated by Nicola Anderson

# What is synthetic phonics?

**Synthetic phonics** teaches children to recognise the sounds of letters and to blend (synthesise) them together to make whole words.

Understanding sound/letter relationships gives children the confidence and ability to read unfamiliar words, without having to rely on memory or guesswork; this helps them to progress towards independent reading.

**Did you know?** Spoken English uses more than 40 speech sounds. Each sound is called a *phoneme*. Some phonemes relate to a single letter (d-o-g) and others to combinations of letters (sh–ar–p). When a phoneme is written down it is called a *grapheme*. Teaching these sounds, matching them to their written form and sounding out words for reading is the basis of synthetic phonics.

# Consultant

*I love reading phonics* has been created in consultation with language expert Abigail Steel. She has a background in teaching and teacher training and is a respected expert in the field of synthetic phonics. Abigail Steel is a regular contributor to educational publications. Her international education consultancy supports parents and teachers in the promotion of literacy skills.

# Reading tips

This book focuses on three sounds made with the letters ea: ee as in eat, e as in bread and ai as in break.

## Tricky words in this book

Any words in bold may have unusual spellings or are new and have not yet been introduced.

> Tricky words in this book:
>
> **mother two one goes brother learn through because**

## Extra ways to have fun with this book

After the reader has read the story, ask them questions about what they have just read:

*Can you remember three words that contain the different sounds shown by the letters ea?*

*Who did Clumsy Eagle trip and land on at the beach?*

Oh dear! Here comes Clumsy Eagle! I hope he doesn't crash into me!

# A pronunciation guide

This grid contains the sounds used in the stories in levels 4, 5 and 6 and a guide on how to say them. /a/ represents the sounds made, rather than the letters in a word.

| | | | |
|---|---|---|---|
| /ai/ as in game | /ai/ as in play/they | /ee/ as in leaf/these | /ee/ as in he |
| /igh/ as in kite/light | /igh/ as in find/sky | /oa/ as in home | /oa/ as in snow |
| /oa/ as in cold | /y+oo/ as in cube/ music/new | long /oo/ as in flute/ crew/blue | /oi/ as in boy |
| /er/ as in bird/hurt | /or/ as in snore/ oar/door | /or/ as in dawn/ sauce/walk | /e/ as in head |
| /e/ as in said/any | /ou/ as in cow | /u/ as in touch | /air/ as in hare/ bear/there |
| /eer/ as in deer/ here/cashier | /t/ as in tripped/ skipped | /d/ as in rained | /j/ as in gent/ gin/gym |
| /j/ as in barge/hedge | /s/ as in cent/ circus/cyst | /s/ as in prince | /s/ as in house |
| /ch/ as in itch/catch | /w/ as in white | /h/ as in who | /r/ as in write/rhino |

Sounds this story focuses on are highlighted in the grid.

| /f/ as in phone | /f/ as in rough | /ul/ as in pencil/ hospital | /z/ as in fries/ cheese/breeze |
|---|---|---|---|
| /n/ as in knot/ gnome/engine | /m/ as in welcome /thumb/column | /g/ as in guitar/ghost | /zh/ as in vision/beige |
| /k/ as in chord | /k/ as in plaque/ bouquet | /nk/ as in uncle | /ks/ as in box/books/ ducks/cakes |
| /a/ and /o/ as in hat/what | /e/ and /ee/ as in bed/he | /i/ and /igh/ as in fin/find | /o/ and /oa/ as in hot/cold |
| /u/ and short /oo/ as in but/put | /ee/, /e/ and /ai/ as in eat/ bread/break | /igh/, /ee/ and /e/ as in tie/field/friend | /ou/ and /oa/ as in cow/blow |
| /ou/, /oa/ and /oo/ as in out/ shoulder/could | /i/ and /ai/ as in money/they | /c/ and /s/ as in cat/cent | /y/, /igh/ and /i/ as in yes/sky/myth |
| /g/ and /j/ as in got/giant | /ch/, /c/ and / sh/ as in chin/ school/chef | /er/, /air/ and /eer/ as in earth/bear/ears | /u/, /ou/ and /oa/ as in plough/dough |

Be careful not to add an 'uh' sound to 's', 't', 'p', 'c', 'h', 'r', 'm', 'd', 'g', 'l', 'f' and 'b'. For example, say 'fff' not 'fuh' and 'sss' not 'suh'.

**Mother** Eagle has three little eaglets.

**Two** of them are neat and careful. But **one** of them is not!

Clumsy Eagle wreaks havoc wherever he **goes**.

On the beach he trips and
lands on an unsuspecting seal,
who is not very pleased!

At home, he tears a hole in the nest. He knocks a meal right out of his sister's beak.

"I'm sorry," he says.
"I meant to be more careful!"

Then as he tries to clean
up the mess, he treads on
his **brother**'s head.

"I'm sorry," he says.
"I really did mean to
be careful!"

His mother surveys the nest.
She glances at the beach.

"Oh Clumsy Eagle," she sighs. "I dread the day you **learn** to fly!"

But the big day gets
nearer and nearer.
The weather is ideal.

The sun is gleaming. The sea
is still. Clumsy Eagle perches
shakily on a breaker.

"Please be careful!" his
mother entreats.
"Look straight ahead!"
squeal his siblings.

"Not in my direction!"
pleads the fearful seal.

Clumsy Eagle takes a deep breath. He spreads his wings.

He reaches up to the sky
and leaps...

Wow! Clumsy Eagle weaves
**through** the clouds.
He swoops over the beach.

The onlookers beam with delight
**because**...
Clumsy Eagle is great at flying!

# OVER **48** TITLES IN SIX LEVELS
## Abigail Steel recommends...

### Some titles from Level 4

I love reading phonics **The Circus Mice**
978-1-84898-582-7

I love reading phonics **Monster's Night**
978-1-84898-583-4

I love reading phonics **The Mummy Code**
978-1-84898-585-8

### Some titles from Level 5

I love reading phonics **The Gigantic Bear**
978-1-84898-586-5

I love reading phonics **Celebrity Celia**
978-1-84898-587-2

I love reading phonics **The Cemetery Dance**
978-1-84898-588-9

### Other titles to enjoy from Level 6

I love reading phonics **Hugh is New**
978-1-84898-590-2

I love reading phonics **Bad Zombie Movie**
978-1-84898-592-6

I love reading phonics **Owen the Astronaut**
978-1-84898-593-3

An Hachette UK Company
www.hachette.co.uk

Copyright © Octopus Publishing Group Ltd 2012
First published in Great Britain in 2012 by TickTock, an imprint of Octopus Publishing Group Ltd,
Endeavour House, 189 Shaftesbury Avenue, London WC2H 8JY.
www.octopusbooks.co.uk

ISBN 978 1 84898 591 9

Printed and bound in China
10 9 8 7 6 5 4 3 2 1